TOMAHAWK LEADERSHIP

Physician Alignment Manual

Alvarez & Pike

Foreword by Thomas L. "Tim" Stover, MD, MBA

Dedication

To our wives and children who have lovingly and patiently supported our endeavors.

To the team of dedicated caregivers with whom we work every day.

Note

This book describes our experiences and methods to enhance physician alignment strategies. The opinions expressed herein do not necessarily reflect those of the organizations mentioned. While the examples ("abstracts") used herein are based on actual events, we've changed the names and settings out of respect for those involved.

Table of Contents

Preface

This manual is intended for:

- Leaders of healthcare organizations who would like to better understand the physician/system dynamic.
- Leaders of medical groups who would like to more effectively engage the professionals they serve.
- Leaders who find themselves in poorly performing organizations in need of rapid turnaround.

Healthcare in America is rapidly changing, and with it, so are the relationships between doctors and hospitals. More than ever, both must be aligned at multiple levels to survive and thrive in the modern world. Be it volume, value, retail or hybrid: No payment model can be optimized without properly aligning physician interests with those of the organization. The financial strength of a health system is only as good as the health of its provider group, which will be reflected in its contribution to the system's operating margin.

While many books have been written about "how to handle" situations with physicians, few have directly tied a management style to its rapid financial turnaround.

Inside you'll find how to harness the power of physician alignment through an action-oriented style of management called **Tomahawk Leadership**. As described by a physician leader, Ben Alvarez, and a healthcare executive, Jeff Pike, you'll learn how to effectively employ its tenets within your hospital's employed physician group to positively impact the system's bottom line and energize your alignment strategies.

Acknowledgements

Nobody works in a vacuum, and progress is the result of the hard work of many. As leadership, we provide vision, direction, and support to our directors, office managers, and staff. We also listen to and empower our physicians to help drive change. All of these extraordinary people are integral to this story.

In addition, we are blessed with having strong boards who took a chance on us and our unorthodox style during difficult times; our CEO, Tim Stover, MD, a maverick and visionary in the area of health and wellness, who trusts us to do "our thing"; our COO, Alan Papa, a brilliant tactician, who teaches us to always think in 360 degrees about doctor relationships and the importance of strategic sequencing; and our fellow senior executives who oftentimes shake their heads at our methods, but still support us.

Last but not least, a special thanks to our Directors, all Tomahawk leaders in their own right, who know how to work hard and laugh much: Adam Gruly, Amy Miller, Greg Podges, Jeff Kovacs,

Mat Gaug, Susan McGrath and Ted Johnson. Thanks, gang.

Ben Alvarez, MD, FACOG, MBA, CPE, JD
Jeff Pike, RN, MHA

Foreword

Tomahawk Leadership: Physician Alignment Manual. A very unusual title for a book on leadership, but I know the authors, and the title is very appropriate for the methods they used to turn around a dysfunctional hospital-owned physician group.

This dyad of an accomplished doc leader and an experienced clinical operations executive were given two directives: Improve the operations and grow the group.

They have done both in less than two years using Tomahawk Leadership. The name is the creation of the doc; it describes his personality and his leadership style. He never uses the tomahawk, but everyone knows it is ever present. He and his vice president always act in the right way to get things done.

Reading this short book will show the reader what is meant by the title, but more than that, it will describe a very effective leadership style.

Thomas L. "Tim" Stover, MD, MBA
CEO and President, Akron General Health System

Introduction

Leading and comporting yourself with courage, a constant sense of urgency, truth and service. We call it Tomahawk Leadership, an action-oriented management style that cuts down to the bone of any matter quickly.

Healthcare organizations today are experiencing changes of biblical proportions, and at the core of every hospital system are the doctors. Without them, all you'd have is empty buildings. Failure to respond quickly to market changes has already left a slew of dead systems, and many of the survivors are barely alive. Thriving systems have decided to thrive. They've acted on well-developed strategic plans fueled by pure will. There's no such thing as "destined to fail". In fact, it's often a choice *not* to prevail, not to do whatever it takes. We took a struggling physician group and turned it around in a year by adding some "tomahawk" to it, and in so doing enabled a hospital system's commitment to its communities into the future.

The book is divided into two sections. The first, **"Tomahawk Leadership"**, reviews the essence of this style, one we've developed over years of experience. The second, "**Applied Tomahawk Leadership**", takes the example our employed physician group, and how we transformed it from a loose association of doctors into a high-functioning productive cohesive group in noticeably short order. Contained herein are **35 real-life examples called** "**abstracts**", which have been sufficiently de-identified to respect our colleagues' privacy while preserving the educational message. These tell the story of what we did, and how we did it.

Although every chapter has been an intensely collaborative effort between both authors, you'll sometimes notice different writing styles depending upon the contributor's background (which you could probably decipher without our help). We intentionally wanted these very different perspectives to come through to the reader, hence the separate section headings of **"The Doc" and "The Business Guy"**---very dissimilar attitudes and personalities, but together extremely effective. The commonality? We're both very direct because time matters on a personal and business level.

We understand that the management style described herein may not appeal to some. However, if you look at successful entrepreneurs, they've succeeded by moving in a straight-line course of action towards their objectives. If you think your organization is functioning well, great. We're saying it could probably work better and get results faster, especially when time is of the essence in a rapidly-evolving industry. Talk a problem to death or take action now. It is a matter of choice. At the end of the day, ethically driven results are what matter, and nobody can mess with success.

THE DOC:
TOMAHAWK LEADERSHIP

Chapter 1. Quality vs. Revenue

You might gather from the book's first few pages that it's about applying a certain management style to achieve desired financial results. That's partly true. However, quality and patient safety are more important. How we take care of patients comes first. Like many in management, especially as the president of the physician group, every morning I compose a new task list to keep track of what I need to do. At the very top, though, I start with "Mission". I always try to connect to---or sometimes gain personal clarity on--- how my work and decisions relate back to my organization's mission.

Our health system, Akron General, in Akron, Ohio, is a tertiary care center that has been in existence for over 100 years. It's a special place because of the many wonderful caring people who work here. Our mission statement, which guides us, is probably very similar to that of most healthcare organizations:

"To improve the health and lives of the people and communities we serve."

I am a physician in a management job. I know that, and it drives my perspective on what I do daily. The reality is sometimes my job can be schizophrenic due to the competing priorities of each. The only truth I know is that if I do what's right by the patient, I'm good. I've also been blessed to have worked in great organizations in my career who have lived their missions: Mt. Sinai (Cleveland, OH); Family Medical Center (Little Falls, MN); Cleveland Clinic (Cleveland, OH); and Akron General (Akron, Ohio) where I'm at presently. They walk the talk and do whatever it takes to help patients and their communities. I believe this is because they've all got docs leading at the top, so patients come first. The University of Tennessee Physician Executive MBA program, where I received my business degree, espouses this very philosophy.

Quality and patient safety were not an issue when Jeff Pike (vice president) and I assumed leadership of Akron General's employed physician group,

Partners Physician Group (PPG). In fact, we were the recognized community leaders in quality, top of mind in our market for "where to receive healthcare." Our issue was lack of a coordinated approach to healthcare delivery with our physician partners. We had great building blocks, lots of good intentions, but little purposeful direction. It was time for a new approach.

PPG needed operational guidance and fast. We employed what evolved to be called Tomahawk Leadership out of necessity, primarily to get the group running cohesively as quickly as possible. The quality had always been there. If you don't have that, no leadership style on earth is going to be effective.

Patients vote mostly with their feet and go where they and their loved ones will get the best care. If quality care is your problem, you are unfortunately in a much more dire situation than the one we faced and will see a stampede of patients to your competitor. Resolving systemic quality concerns will require leadership changes, a complete re-tooling of services, critical assessment of weak service lines, and/or strategic alliances with higher-quality providers. Therefore, make quality and patient safety the preeminent concerns. Live your mission, and the patients will come.

Chapter 2. Tomahawk Leadership

Tomahawk Leadership is leading with "tomahawk in hand". It involves courage, straight talk, and saying what needs to be said to whom it needs saying **immediately**. It requires a servant attitude with an edge. It involves respect. It's about looking to the future, not dwelling on useless life-sucking refuse past. It also requires acknowledging that failure is assured if dramatic action is not taken. It means facing challenges head-on---that you may have intentionally provoked--- to get a job done. It entails people understanding that you won't back down, and that you mean business. For all this, you've got to dig deep. It is not easy. But it is most crucial when a company's survival is in question, and you're dealing with intelligent, driven professionals in the midst of an industry's revolution---like doctors and healthcare.

Abstract #1. Challenge the premise. You're in a meeting and someone makes the statement, "We're doing all we can to fix the issue". Problem is: Everyone around the table knows it's not true, either from a lack of capacity or effort. You say, "Tell me what the immovable roadblocks are, those you believe cannot be overcome." They begin to list them. You ask, "Why?" and discover focused conversations have NOT been had with specific doctors on staff regarding patient flow issues because that doc would "have a fit". You say, "Great, I'll talk to him." You do, get some resistance, but issue resolved. You tell your team, "Most of our limitations are self-induced---get out of your own way."

All too often we see teams fail because obvious problems and associated personalities go untouched for fear of conflict. Personally, though, I've never gotten into it with anybody who didn't have it coming, and I sure don't lose sleep over it. The trick is deliberately directing your force in a way that furthers your objectives.

Precision in the wielding of your tomahawk is what you want----this is business at its core---hitting metrics, well-defined targets. All you need is conviction and a clear understanding of, "I'm doing what I was hired to do. I'm doing my job". You're on a mission, maybe even a very diplomatic and professional warpath, depending upon the situation. Flex your style to getting real with people and get going right now.

I've had colleagues comment on the "aggressive nature" of this approach. It sounds aggressive, but it is not. It is firm, focused, respectful, professional and effective. I remind them that although the tomahawk has historically been used as a fighting tool, it's also a symbol of peace and coming together --- and there's no shorter path to these than clarity of message and active engagement, the struggle that unites people working towards similar goals. Again, it's about leadership pushing a mission forward when time matters.

Here are the **Core Principles of Tomahawk Leadership, which we term C.U.T.S.:**

- **Courage**
- **Urgency**
- **Truth**
- **Service**

Let's look at each of the **C.U.T.S.** principles in more depth.

COURAGE

Courage is an act of will. It's a decision. It's doing something despite knowing you're putting yourself at risk in some way. It's looking fear in the eye and saying, "Bring it". You want to run, but you don't.

Abstract #2. Disruptive physicians. It seems every place has a few. Their behaviors, which can be extremely destructive, have usually never been addressed, and if they have, they've been ineffective due to lack of consequences. So, Dr. Bully acts out in public with me. I remain calm, let him finish, and ask him to accompany me to my office. There I proceed to tell him, "You've just triggered our disruptive physician policy; and, by the way, if you refuse to participate in the process, which includes mandatory anger-management counseling, you'll be terminated <u>with cause</u> (painful, and one he'll be explaining for years to come to licensing boards and employers)." In my experience, abusive personalities can rarely be rehabilitated, so, don't negotiate. I make sure to always document the conversation, give the doc a copy as a *keepsake, and put one in his/her employment file. In this case, he successfully went through the process and changed his behavior.*

We see courage displayed on battlefields, in the streets, in families and patients. It's all around. We see it in business, too. Without it there would be no progress. Too often organizations fail to move forward for lack of it. Funny thing is, though, it doesn't take much. After all, we're not talking about facing down an oncoming tank. We're talking about opening your mouth about the problems and people who are holding your organization back and pushing past these obstacles. It might take saying things just once, but it usually involves repetitive strikes at the issue, chipping away to the point where people get on board or get out of your way.

"Army of One" stuff? Yes and no. The courage to promote change comes from an individual, which usually helps instill courage in others to join the cause. I like to say "One leads to an army". Enlist your brothers and sisters for support. Backing is imperative, and you're going to need a lot of it, because the Tomahawk style may make you slightly controversial. Be ready to be psychologically analyzed a-la "You've got issues". I know, because I've seen it happen to many on our team, including me. Don't worry, have faith. After all, you *are* doing your job, and in so doing are saving the jobs of others. If you're lucky enough to have a few key senior leader compadres who understand that rapid change is essential for mission success, you're good. If not, then say what needs saying and let the chips fall where they may. There are always powerful and successful reality-based people in any enterprise who have been waiting for someone like you to come along and make things happen. They will support and appreciate your efforts.

Does it take more guts to deal with highly educated people like doctors? I don't think so. As a whole, we're intense, but we're human, too. With any professionals you've got to be on your game and armed with data.

You have to tell them what you expect in no uncertain terms. One-on-one or as a group, they can be intimidating, but don't back down. Meet frequently with whom you're trying to influence on whatever turf makes sense. Use all available technology to communicate; bring them into the conversation. Despite your best efforts, you'll still hear the familiar cries of, " We had no input!" Remain calm and re-engage in a timely and direct fashion, making sure they're able to articulate your message back to you. Also, keep in mind that people have competing priorities, so help them focus on their job of taking care of patients. Repetitive messaging works. But **you** have got to speak up, zero in on your mission, and press on.

URGENCY

Urgency means at every moment you're on edge about your objectives, constantly with tomahawk in hand. That's how you need to roll. It's about never letting up, never stopping, never taking your eyes off the competition. It's looking forward beyond the bend. Constant motion. Constant agitation. Constant disruption. Constant pressure.

Abstract #3. What are you waiting for? I had been at the helm of the provider group a little over 3 months, still getting my bearings. The system's outlook wasn't good, and the losses were terrible, the projections even worse. An idea had been gingerly discussed for years: Ask the doctors to keep things in-system. A lot of talk about it, plenty of vetting, no action. I walked into a board meeting and gently announced a plan to reduce leakage effective immediately (described later in the book). No more contemplation. Action and resolve. I made myself, one person, the object of those who would resist. No confusion about the message or intent. Every day of delay would worsen our position and threaten the mission. The results: System turn-around (see Chapter 12, "Results").

Call them "Type A" personalities, or whatever you like, but you'll need a coalition of such like-minded people if you are to move your organizational mountain. You must quickly make an honest assessment of yourself and existing team members, hire or borrow others, and assign some out if they don't fit the bill. Remember, we're talking about effecting *rapid* change, so, no time for emotional vacillation on your part. Hire who you need to hire; fire who you need to fire. If you don't, you'll get nowhere. Once your team is assembled, it's up to you to set the example and the pace.

Regarding tomahawks and scalping: Do not be afraid to take a few scalps and wear them on your belt (figuratively, of course). Every organization has legacy under-performers or "inhibitors". These people are recognized by all as, "Yeah, that's the way he/she's always been." Really? If there's no improvement forthcoming, get rid of them AND disseminate throughout the organization why they were let go. This more than anything captures people's attention and raises consciousness exponentially.

Beware the self-induced disease of Consultant Paralysis. It usually strikes when issues perceived as serious arise, and credibility is an issue. Most leaders usually know what needs to be done, but might feel they need validation from an external source ("a consultant is a highly-paid expert from out of town"). Hopefully, you've got plenty of smart people in your own company. We do. Listen to what they're saying and help them be heard. Nothing can bring momentum to a grinding halt like hiring a consultant whose analyses can take months to complete. Nobody knows your terrain like you do. Save yourself precious time and money and have the intelligent people around you find solutions and execute on them.

TRUTH

Just say it. Tell people the truth. You'll be saving everyone a lot of time and effort. Some sensitive souls may not like it, but again, you have to do what is necessary to get your job done as quickly as possible. Remember, this is about acting a certain way because the organization either turns around or falters. Vary your delivery style, blunt or soft, depending upon with whom you're speaking and the situation. Listen first, read the other person's temperature, then start talking.

Abstract #4. The "Options Talk". I've had physicians whose contracts call for a guaranteed salary for a specific term followed by a production compensation model. We'll do this to give them time to build a practice if they're just starting out. We also watch this closely as sometimes guarantees can lead to a relaxed physician attitude about work, e.g.,

"Why should I work hard---I'm getting paid no matter what." Canceling patients, taking a lot of time off, not working full-time, and "administrative days" tip us off to this mentality. This leads to encouragement discussions. If their efforts remain underwhelming, and they are unmoved by our recurrent talks, I meet with them and present two options: a) A contract amendment in which they'll go on to a production model if no noticeable change is seen in 3 months or b) They can leave the organization. Some may say it's not much of an option, but it's their choice to get with it or not, and at least I'm giving them a chance. To date, most docs have stayed and been quite successful, and a few have even thanked me for the "wake-up call".

For those who love "secret sauces", this happens to be it: Speaking the truth. Without it, none of the suggestions in this book will be effective. Be mindful, though, of where you speak the truth just as much as how you speak it. For example, I always deliver sensitive messages to doctors in-person and one-on-one. I talk plainly, pulling no punches. In private they don't have to worry about saving face before others. So, I avoid an audience. Tell them exactly what's on your mind and precisely what consequences they can expect if certain behaviors persist. Also, make sure the blinds to your office are open during this dialogue. Transparency to the outside world helps keep emotions in check and protects you, too. Dealing with a duplicitous character? That's when I have someone in there with me as a witness. If the physician or colleague becomes disrespectful, the meeting is over. You are done and tell him so: "I'm done with this conversation". Deploy your Disruptive Physician/Employee policy (if your organization doesn't have one, develop one fast). Don't tolerate abuse or get drawn into a fight unless it's deliberate and serves your specific purpose. If anyone becomes threatening, pick up the phone and call security. Again, you mean business, and people will need to understand that very quickly. When others lose it, keep your cool. You control the encounter.

SERVICE

Be the model of servant leadership to your executive team. Make clear your expectations surrounding whom they're serving, and the speed at which this needs to occur. There is a goal here, and the way your team approaches deliverables requires a "team tomahawk" state of mind. You all run at the same speed. If anyone has trouble keeping up, provide help and guidance. If incorrigible, they have to go. You cannot do it alone, so everyone needs to be on the same page. Surround yourself with talent and fast. Trust to build trust. After a short period of deletions and additions, we quickly developed a management team of highly motivated, self-disciplined and effective leaders. It is they who live in the trenches of the physician group and effect what needs to happen.

Abstract #5. I'm an Ob/Gyn. In my mind, the physician group is under my care, just like my patients. I work for them. I am obliged to them, at their beck and call 24/7 no matter where I may be on earth. If they need me, I'm there, and they've got no stronger ally in their corner. If they call, text, or e-mail me, I respond the same day whenever humanly possible. In my opinion, to not do so is professionally unacceptable. Remember, though, your administrative team members may not see the world as you do. They weren't "raised" that way. You yourself, then, better be walking the talk if others are to follow--- and explicitly communicate your expectations, as I had to do shortly after arriving at Akron General.

Emphasize constantly your organization's mission. Abide by it. It's the higher-purpose for what you do, that to which everyone should be committed. It's the beacon in the fog that keeps you on the right track. I remind my crew that it's like climbing a mountain where we're all on the same rope team. A successful summit attempt becomes possible only when we understand we're dependent upon each other to get to the top and back down safely. A weak link can literally kill you. Trust me, I've been on some pretty challenging mountains and have even fallen into a crevasse on Mt. Rainier. On another occasion I got high-altitude pulmonary edema while ascending Denali. Effective teamwork is why I'm alive today. What about the elements of your mission you cannot control, i.e., those who are tasked to support you, but don't share your sense of urgency, thereby hindering, usually inadvertently, your progress?

This can be challenging but will improve as you show results. Keep at it. Help them understand a new dynamic is in play. Nothing works better than dogged determination.

Chapter 3. Effectiveness

We know Tomahawk Leadership works because we saw it rapidly transform a medical group that, for multiple reasons, had been limping along for years. Then the explosive results came. Don't take my word for it. See the Chapter 12, "Results", and decide for yourself.

Abstract #6. The Red Folder. I like being prepared for any bluffs or threats a provider may throw my way. I just assume that if someone is coming to negotiate in bad faith, they already have a plan B of what they are going to do when it doesn't go their way. For example, I've had docs on occasion threaten to leave the group if I don't give in to some unreasonable demand. For these occasions, I have a red folder within arms reach in my office with pre-printed copies of letters for them to sign which state, "I hereby give 90 days notice without cause that I'll be leaving the group." I calmly and respectfully hand them one, tell them it would be sad to see them go, but I would understand--- and to just think about it carefully for a few days before taking such a big step. I always try to let them save face and leave the door open to a continued relationship, which is what tends to happen most of the time. Once they get their bearings, the effective dialogue begins.

Ultimately, achievement should be the focus, not how hard people try. We've all experienced meetings where an individual's effort was solemnly celebrated in the setting of failure. This tends to be the hallmark of a benign culture and soft leadership, where interpersonal relationships supersede accountability. It's being nice at the expense of success.

Abstract #7. Measure to discover. There is a huge but often overlooked divide between "Effort" and "Outcome". When we first started, there appeared to be a lot of effort work going on by all parties in our management team. No one person stuck out as being lazy, duplicitous, or incapable, yet not much was actually getting done. Once a strategic plan was created, we developed outcomes-oriented scorecards for each manager. Based on measurable results, it became readily apparent that one director in particular was largely ineffective at achieving the established goals and had to be replaced. It wasn't until we began analytically evaluating outcomes rather than perceived effort that we were able to separate a winning team from those that were holding it back.

Our team spends the majority of its time on the road in over 80 office locations spread out across 30 square miles. Lacking the in-person oversight most work environments provide, management had historically promoted people that they liked on a personal level. Nice people who appeared smart and engaged in meetings rose through the ranks and were continually rewarded despite poor performance in the group. We changed that routine quickly.

Another important note on using outcomes-based measurement: It might help you discover quiet superstars in your midst. We recently promoted a manager (Greg P.) to director who was largely overlooked by previous management. Greg is by nature more introverted, but not to the point where he doesn't speak. He just talks when he's got something to say. It wasn't until we started looking at the impact he had on the financial performance of our most cohesive and successful group, Akron General Orthopedics, that we realized what we had. Consequently, we were able to identify a truly skilled "go-to guy" leader by his remarkable accomplishments.

To get a tough job done rapidly and right you need:

- A plan
- Personal involvement
- Support from the top
- Courage to make decisions
- Competent team members
- Commitment to endure the heat

By applying C.U.T.S., we were able to strengthen the physician group, which led directly to extraordinary increases in contribution margin to the system. No rocket science, just guts, committed smart people, and honest appreciation of human nature. These same ingredients of achievement can be applied to any business. Paint your face and grab your tomahawk. Will it be easy? No. Will there be resistance? Absolutely. Just remember resistance means you've touched a nerve. There's life in that limb. Make it move. Disruption of the status quo is a resurrecting force.

Chapter 4. The Problem

Most underperforming groups tend to suffer from deep-rooted unaddressed maladies, legacies of, "We've always done it that way", "Nobody ever told me", or "Who cares". **The problem is weak leadership**. Poor leadership allows poor leaders to lead poorly. In today's competitive environment, there's just no place for it. Change yourself first if you are to change the program, or you'll find yourself transitioned out.

Abstract #8. Help others lead better. I'm blessed to be working with the most intelligent group of people I've ever known. One of them is our Director of Finance (Jeff K.). This kid is brilliant, affable, honest and knows how to talk to doctors. Early on I noticed we had a disconnect about response time to physicians' inquiries. I wanted answers stat; his analyses as a matter of course take time. It was my fault, though. I had not spoken to him about my expectations (yet I expected him to read my mind). Once I did, we both got on the same page. Now, he is an even bigger rock star whose natural talents I know will take him far. It's not easy, but always ask yourself if you're part of the problem you're trying to solve.

Abstract #9. Be a mentor. Jeff Pike, the "business guy", co-author of this book, and my Vice President, is good-hearted, great at business, and plainspoken. Some doctors did not respond well to his style and misinterpreted some of his words as disrespectful. However, I saw a clarity of thought, the likes of which you notice in just a few people along your career. He needed mentoring, specifically on <u>how</u> to address doctors. So, I asked him to observe my interactions with physicians and gave him a view into a doc's mind. Over a few months he totally changed his message delivery and is now much more successful at engaging the docs effectively.

In the healthcare delivery debate it seems that doctors get blamed for a lot because we're "too individualistic". This might be partly true, but remember that our focus is the patient, not the business. Doctors need guidance with respect. Why? Because of the training, effort, delayed gratification, and sacrifices we've endured to get to where we are. Physicians, like all other highly trained professionals, have earned a certain badge of honor. This, of course, does not justify bad behaviors, but it would serve you well to regard this hard-earned, sometimes-not-so-subtle, attitude of entitlement carefully. No matter what changes the future may bring to healthcare, this characteristic will probably persist unless medical schools and residencies become a breeze. So, be respectful and vigilant of every word you utter at every encounter. You really don't need a perceived insult getting in the way of what you're trying to accomplish.

Individualism isn't a bad thing. In fact, great ideas mostly start with one person, who must then enlist a team to help move it forward. Physician groups generally tend to be low on team spirit because each one is focused on doing his/her innumerable tasks, many of which unfortunately have nothing to do with patient care. When physician groups are experiencing lack-luster performance, it probably relates back to this in some way. You need to help them do their jobs, get them engaged with each other and moving in the same direction.

Bottom line: Physicians are not irrational beings, so put away preconceived assumptions and don't back away from them. Give them their due respect and let them help you. Put tomahawks in their hands, too. Empower them in disrupting the equilibrium. You've all got a job to do together. No choice here.

In the next sections we'll outline what needs to happen right now, Tomahawk Leadership style, if your group/team/hospital system, etc. are to get out of their present abyss and excel in the future.

Chapter 5. Why must I do anything *right now?*

Of course, none of us has to do anything except that which fulfills a physiologic need. However, if you don't get your team unified and moving in the right direction post-haste, especially when your organization is in a nose-dive, what follows is the "reality sequence", no matter what job or industry you're in.

Reality Sequence:

1. Financial losses mount.
2. No capital for growth and mission support.
3. Lay-offs.
4. Reduced services.
5. The local paper publicizes the lay-offs and reduced services.
6. Patients perceive quality as sub-standard.
7. Patients go elsewhere.
8. Volumes tank.
9. Losses increase.
10. Good doctors leave.

11. Recruiting new ones becomes difficult.
12. The community loses access to medical care.
13. The CFO becomes more unhappy than usual.
14. The CEO wonders whether you're the right person for the job.
15. The Board starts to think the same thing.
16. You shall---and should--- be fired.

Abstract #10. First you want to stone us, now you're singing our praises. When the going gets tough, instead of the "tough get going" a lot of people tend to get edgy. As I've indicated before, we inherited a quality physician group devoid of operational effectiveness. It was my impression that the system CFO expected overnight success. She was impatient and, truth be told, she had guts, was a strong supporter, but wanted results "yesterday". Along the way we endured some heat, but most of our senior leaders, especially our CEO and COO, encouraged us to stay the course. One month in particular we were grilled about our finances. The next month, almost a year to the day of our coming on board, the group's contribution margin to the system exploded. It was so dramatic, that the finance department had to go back and check the numbers. They were correct. Now, in a sudden reversal, my team and I were being lauded. Lesson learned: If you think you're doing the right thing, press on.

From a practical standpoint, money enables mission, because without it, no business can deliver unto its customers what they want and need in a sustained fashion. Ultimately, if you can't keep the lights on, it's game over.

By imposition, healthcare is moving rapidly towards value-based "better-not-more" medicine, but it's not fully here yet. We can talk value all we want, but we're still going to have to deliver value to enough patients to enable hospital systems to care for the populations they serve. If a group is not tight and behaving like a team, it will be unable to meet the challenges for getting paid in an outcomes-driven reimbursement model. As such, it is imperative to have a group working together to succeed in quality-based healthcare. Laying the foundation of group performance now will allow this transition in the near future---and by looking at the speed of change sweeping the industry, organizations must prepare now. To merely react will not suffice.

Chapter 6. Flexibility, Adaptability and Speed

Doing what you said you would do by when you said you'd do it (my favorite "Stoverism"). Nothing is more powerful to establish trust. It is belief in the other person's integrity based upon a series of promises kept that maintains the relationship--- much more than any contract can. It's also crucial during rocky times. Deals are sealed by people.

If you're the one in your organization tasked with physician alignment, remember that you're on stage 24/7. You are the one who is continuously being interviewed. Every discussion, comment, joke, gesture, e-mail, or deal you make is telegraphing to everyone who you are. The best scenario is when you're being yourself. Phonies usually are obvious and held in contempt. If your actions have led physicians at large to believe you are untrustworthy, you are finished--- go find another job. We spoke earlier about being truthful as the secret sauce. Seeing is believing, so people better be seeing you're a straight arrow, or your alignment efforts will fall short.

Successful physician alignment depends upon demonstrating flexibility, adaptability and speed. Today's challenges are great, as are the opportunities. "Necessity is the mother of invention". This has been the theme at Akron General for as long as anyone can remember. Without question we have been the market leaders in innovative business strategies because we've had to be. We've been mobile and agile, but never hostile; and **we've worked our strategic plan**.

At PPG, we've listened to what physicians want, which essentially comes down to 2 things:

1. Let me take care of patients in peace.
2. Pay me fairly for the work I do.

Our response to these has been, "Ok, let's work together to see how we can get there." Human decision-making is complex, as is what motivates people (more about this in Chapter 11, "Alignment Models"). Cookie-cutter approaches to doc deals may appeal to some, but when standing in a competitive field, he who can best adapt and deliver a personalized "alignment package" which satisfies the individual's needs will take the day. During these discovery discussions, it's important to be fastidious about response time. Don't let an alignment talk cool, as it can be interpreted as disinterest. Maintain contact, but don't harangue either. Be responsive to a fault. Keep e-mails to a minimum---pick up the phone or meet instead. You're developing a relationship. Surprise them with extraordinary attentiveness. My mentor and friend, Dr. Irwin Kornbluth, taught me, "Relationships continue as they begin." Help the physicians see a mutually-beneficial future based upon their experiences with you now. In the next section, we'll describe some of the physician model options we used to grow our system.

Abstract #11. Give them something STAT. We've got a great relationship with our in-house legal team, which is quite important. One of our recent colleagues (Barb S.) would always remind us, "The lawyer is your friend." It's true. They've got reams of paper to review and are usually buried under them. When we came to Akron General, the legal corps consisted of a skeleton crew, which resulted in a significant

lag time in getting contracts to doctors. This delay, in turn, was oftentimes interpreted by the docs as disinterest, or worse, disorganization--- both the kiss of death for any deal. Our attorneys needed help, so we worked together on developing a "term sheet". These are not binding contracts, but rather a 2 page document that outlines the major points of the deal, like compensation, term (duration), non-compete clause, benefits, CME, etc. We were now able to immediately hand doctors concrete proof that we meant business. After reaching agreement, we'd then return the term sheets to legal for them to plug into actual contract templates. No more delays. Because of the high trust level, we were able to help each other.

Abstract #12. Pick up the phone. Have you ever been in the situation where you're waiting to make a decision because someone in your organization is waiting on someone else for crucial information? You e-mail, call and meet with your people, but "We're waiting on Joe Blow to get back to me." Solution: Pick up the phone yourself and call Joe. There's nothing like injecting yourself personally into the matter.

Like my dad used to always say," If you're the interested one, then do something about it".

What about when a deal you've been working on for months goes south inexplicably? How do you handle this alignment dilemma? You will surely be disappointed, but do not take it personally. In fact, if you expect it, it'll soften the emotional toll. We can only take people at their word, so try to assume good will and positive intentions. There might be a few reasons the other party pulled out. They could be afraid. They could be using you as leverage for a better deal. They could lack trust. They're not ready for a change. They've been threatened with legal action by whomever they're leaving. If dealing with a group, perhaps all the partners are not on board. In these sudden reversals, it's best to let them walk away with dignity. Don't get angry. Don't debate. Don't call the next day and try to get them back to the table. Let them off graciously and wish them luck. Remember: If you were willing to do a deal with them now, maybe there'll be a deal in the future. Leave things as amicably and open as possible.

In the next section, "The Business Guy: Applied Tomahawk Leadership", we'll show what it's like to translate the four C.U.T.S. principles into meaningful action and results. Again, this leadership style is one predicated on constant motion and commotion. No gold stars for trying, only for succeeding. We'll continue using the example of our physician group, PPG, where we wielded the tomahawk with striking success. Although we candidly recognize the hard work of many throughout all levels of the organization, the group's rapid transformation was in large part responsible for our health system's dramatic turn-around and continued viability.

THE BUSINESS GUY: APPLIED TOMAHAWK LEADERSHIP

Chapter 7. In the Beginning

Partners Physician Group ("PPG"), Akron General's employed physician group, had been in existence for approximately 15 yrs. After years of growth, sadly it had gone quiet. Quality doctors, but weak group dynamics and operations. When we took the helm, our marching orders from Dr. Stover, the CEO, were typically clear and direct: Expand the physician group and "fix it". It had roughly 136 providers in about 30 locations--- large but not huge. Multi-specialty by design, it enjoyed most specialties you'd find in a hospital's ambulatory group. Like most, ours was created to support the community. Our health system consists of a 534 bed acute care hospital, one Critical Access hospital in Lodi, Ohio and various entities in vertical alignment including hospice, rehab, home care, stand-alone emergency departments, ambulatory surgery sites, and three health-and-wellness centers.

The organizational structure of our physician group consists of a board, a president, vice-president, chief medical officer and directors. The number of directors would grow as the number of practices grew. So did the number of support personnel dedicated to PPG, like HR, IT, marketing and finance.

The environment in town was and continues to be extremely competitive with three systems fighting for market share and the attention of a few remaining independent physician practices for alignment. Our health system itself was in the middle of its fourth year in a row of negative margins. The lack of profitability had reduced its ability to refresh aging capital or to make strategic investments in the system's future. Bond ratings had just been reduced leading to more costly borrowing. The last two years had led to sizable gut wrenching reductions-in-force at the hospital.

Competition in our market was approaching lunacy. The year prior we had opened a large ambulatory health-and-wellness center with a stand-alone emergency department in an effort to enhance our presence on the boundary of our market. Four months later our main competitor opened a similar operation a 1/2 mile down the road in a community only needing or able to support one. Their idea of competition was to duplicate our services in every area and outspend us on marketing the endeavor. It was determined that our only hope to secure a stable future was to strategically and dynamically grow physician alignment in the community as fast as possible before competing forces from out-of-town, or those in town, captured further market share through physician acquisition.

PPG was in operational stagnation for many reasons. Managerial and operational controls were decentralized, still residing within the individual practice sites. Compensation models were quite different and depended a lot on the doctors' negotiation ability and relationships. While everyone was within fair market value, it wasn't unusual to have variation within the same specialty with regards to employment agreements. Electronic medical records were more varied than alignment strategies with 10 different EMR's, including paper. Leakage to the competition was rampant within PPG. In fact, some practices sent more patients to our competitors than they did into our own system! Our analytics put leakage numbers in the millions from our primary care groups alone. When physicians were asked why they wouldn't refer a patient within the group or system, physicians would site prior relationships with other physicians, prior access problems within our system, or just plain lack of awareness of who was in their own group.

Office managers within the various practices weren't aligned to any central structure. Some even had clauses in the physician's contract that they couldn't be fired or disciplined. As you might imagine, focused control of practice operations, policies, and managerial direction were extremely challenging. Turning this ship without control of the rudder in the middle of a tempest proved almost overwhelming, terrifying and, seemed, quite frankly, not possible.

The results? Subsidy per provider (loss) was over the national benchmarks; leakage was approximated to be in the millions; no patient centered medical home practices; little centralized control of anything, process or outcome-related; and operational coma.

There is a Change Theory developed by Kurt Lewin in 1947 that is useful to describe what we've seen in the past three years. The basis of the theory is that change is a series of unfreezing, changing, and re-freezing events. The applicability in this case is that our group was indeed frozen. What we needed was an El Niño to unfreeze it so we could create a more stable steady state before freezing it back. That El Niño came in the form of Ben Alvarez, the new president of our group and my co-author. He got the call from our CEO and walked in, day one, with tomahawk in hand. He brought pragmatism, credibility, focus and support for our group's leadership. He set a tone of action disrupting our current state; took control of the situation; and moved it out of its perpetual strategic recruitment phase towards the beginnings of true process alignment. As his vice president, I learned first-hand the importance of who is at the top. He didn't restrain me. Rather, he trusted me and set me loose do what I had to do--- and backed me all the way.

To accomplish what some may consider the impossible, you need the right person at the head. Trust me, they are hard to find, but out there. When you see one in action, you'll know it. Keep close, learn and follow. Such leaders have infectious drive and are hugely effective by the example of their work ethic and steadfastness.

Chapter 8. Physician Alignment Continuum

What exactly is alignment? It means getting "in-line" with the program, pieces and parts working in synchrony. Physician alignment within a healthcare system makes for excellent analysis as a dual dynamic containing two elements: Relational Direction and Business Proposition. It has both a natural continuum and a life cycle no different than any other complex human endeavor. How long that life cycle lasts depends on the organization's ability to maturate two interrelated parties, physicians and hospitals, toward joint vision and value creation. It also means getting creative.

Abstract #13. "I don't want to be employed." How do you align a physician or physician group to your system when they don't need or want to? Many examples exist, some of which have nothing to do with contracts. Sometimes the power of the personal relationship is all that's needed. Creatively, you might offer to lease their services. Dr. Stover figured out exactly how to do that before we assumed leadership of PPG.

Successful independent physicians want above all else to maintain their autonomy and their proven way of running a business. Contractually aligning via a leased model (professional services agreement or PSA, see Chapter 11, "Alignment Models"), however, allows that to continue while providing benefit to both parties. In essence, the group now is "under the tent" and gives both an opportunity to work together. We've had numerous PSA's, many of which have transitioned to employment because the relationship worked, but there is some risk. Be very careful with whom you'd like to align, and have a reputable healthcare attorney at your side when constructing the deal.

You don't have to look too far back to see this dynamic implode. The 90's were rife with hospitals and physicians joining together as business partners only to crumble under their own weight in fairly spectacular fashion. If you've been in healthcare leadership for any length of time, it is almost guaranteed that you have either seen, or been a part of, a failed physician alignment strategy. As you know, these failures are extremely destructive both economically and relationally. So much so, that it's quite surprising that they have resurfaced so quickly within the fabric of the healthcare tapestry.

The key to understanding both the history and the future of physician alignment is to understand the continuum of physician alignment, correctly identifying where in this continuum a group exists, and successfully maneuvering your alignment strategy to create joint vision and value.

In the next several pages, we'll describe the Physician Alignment Continuum itself, where on the continuum our own subject group existed at the start, and where on the continuum we are currently. Continuum progression is a journey not a sprint, and it will take years for any group to achieve it's true potential.

Physician Alignment Continuum

The Physician Alignment Continuum is set against the backdrop of the two components mentioned at the beginning of the chapter: Relational Direction and Business Proposition. At the beginning of the continuum these two components are typically very separate and often not conjoined in any way. As a group matures operationally these two components begin to merge ultimately melding into a symbiotic organism primarily focused on patient care delivery. Let's explore the three phases of Physician Alignment.

Strategic Recruitment

Strategic Recruitment is ultimately about achieving growth, size and clinical need. It's often realized in a competitive environment with multiple health system's vying for the attention and inclusion of formerly independent physicians or physician groups. This phase of physician alignment is oftentimes more dependent on the business proposition that on relational direction. Depending on the competitive nature of the environment, the business proposition is often imbalanced and over-dependent upon the financial mechanics of the deal. In this phase, key indicators like subsidy per physician can be through the roof and relational indicators like care-coordination are slim to non-existent. At its very worst, the hospital gets little more than the ability to include itself on a sign and hand out lab coats with its logos. At it's best, the hospital sees an up-tick in coordination of care between the recruited physician, other members of the group, and the hospital itself. Operationally, however, little if anything has changed at the physician office other than billing and signage. Electronic medical records, system navigation, scheduling, practice management, and referral patterns remain nearly or exactly the same as they were before acquisition of the practice into the health system's group.

Abstract #14. "We're independent." Physicians value their independence greatly. There are so many constraints, however, on the practice of medicine by so many parties, that it's really an illusion. When we assumed leadership of PPG and went around to visit the practices, we were surprised at the number of doctors in the group who actually referred to themselves as being "in private practice". We even had some asking if they could work for a competing system. So low were we on group identity, that when reminded they were under contract with us, some were incredulous. We remedied this with refresher conversations about the provenance of their paychecks.

Another key dynamic of this phase is lack of standardized financial mechanics and compensation models throughout the group. It's likely that in order to grow in size, individual negotiations have led to a myriad of contract parameters not all of which truly help tie the physician's success to that of the group or hospital. Quality-based metrics may be in place but are still in their infantile stage surrounding care delivered in the office (like vaccinations or hand-washing), but have little to do with true patient-centered care-coordination throughout the system like chronic care-management or transitions-of-care.

This phase is characterized by variation in compensation amongst like specialties under varying productivity levels. It is nearly impossible to systemically move the group in a singular direction utilizing financial incentives because too much variation exists. As stated, physicians in this phase still see themselves as largely independent of the whole. They have joined a group to gain financial stability but haven't truly incorporated themselves, nor envision themselves, as integral to the success of the whole. Like dipping one's toes in the pool without diving in, they find relief from the heat without truly swimming toward success. Autonomy is highly valued in this phase because physicians naturally require it and haven't yet seen that giving it up can make anything operationally better for them or their patients beyond, of course, the financial security they negotiated prior to joining the hospital.

Process Alignment

Process Alignment is about group coordination, standardization of office and system processes and data integration. In this phase the group begins three very important transformations. The first of these is building a group identity. In this phase you have the beginning of physician engagement. The main objective here is to convince the individuals to wear the T-shirt. Doctors in this phase begin to understand and know each other on-sight. Committees exist that enable them to interact and join in group-decision making. Referral patterns and relationships build. Ironically, as management you can identify this phase in the form of complaints around care delivery and access: "I sent my patient to Dr. So-and-So, and my patient couldn't get in for a week". In this phase physicians are still looking for a reason to remain autonomous, which in turn creates tension as they begin to interact with an imperfect system.

Abstract #15. Vacations. Nothing is more sacrosanct to physicians than time-off, and this needs monitoring through a standardized process. One of the first things we did when we assumed leadership of the group was to institute a rule that all physician time-off would require 30-day notice via a request form. That form would then need approval from the office manager, director, VP and President. We did this primarily for the patient, as too many emergent vacations were affecting patient care. Secondarily, running an office requires planning. This seemingly reasonable policy was met with much disdain. However, it represented the opening salvo in the struggle towards process standardization for the group as a whole.

The second transformation of this phase surrounds office and system processes. A group in this phase either has or is working towards a standardized revenue cycle. Co-pays and unpaid cash collections, scheduling systems, call centers, posting and billing all begin to normalize around system level policies and departments. In this phase the group's financial operations coalesce into centralized departments staffed by specialists, not generalists, as formerly utilized at the practice level. For a leader, this group transformation may be the most important. This is *the* proving ground, the test by which a physician's need for autonomy can either be mitigated or entrenched. To return to the pool analogy, your physicians are now waist-high in the pool, inching in, arms poised tentatively above the water, making the final determination on whether to commit and go under or head back to the side of the pool.

The third and final transformation of this phase surrounds the electronic medical record, the practice management system, and data integration. In this phase the group standardizes around the electronic platform. Systems are put in place to ensure care documentation gains visibility throughout the group. This integration of data goes beyond simple results-reporting and evolves toward patient and disease tracking. Once successfully completed, the group can identify key patient indicators and follow care throughout their referral continuum. Primary care physicians can utilize the system to both schedule patients with specialists as well as identify the care path utilized by the specialist once the patient is returned to them. Key in this phase is that the patient actually returns to the primary care physician once the acute or specialized need has been resolved. The hospital electronic system becomes a large piece of this phase as well. At a minimum physicians are notified once patients leave the acute setting; more desirable, the physician is notified when they arrive at the hospital and can view the patients' care plan upon discharge.

Integrated Care Delivery

Integrated Care Delivery is about the sum of the group working better than the former conglomerate of individual practices for both the patient and clinician. In this phase, the group has achieved singular and transparent documentation systems, results reporting, and primary care notification. Care delivery is more coordinated with a focus on the patient's care transitions. In this phase, outcomes are not only improving but the health system has the ability to track that they are improving. The provision of coordinated ambulatory medicine reduces the frequency of acute episodes decreasing overall costs for the patient. Leakage out-of-system issues, so prevalent in former phases, diminish as practice management systems, enhanced scheduling, and electronic information-sharing create an environment where referring the patient within system is better not only for the patient, but for the physician and physician's staff, too. In this phase, the group can begin tapping into secondary pay sources like transitions-in-care, patient centered medical home, chronic care management, and quality pay-for-performance programs (value-based). Medicare Shared Savings plans can also be considered within this phase but utilize your analytics to join this cause once your outcomes warrant participation.

Abstract #16. Call center. By the time this manual gets published, we'll be well down the

road to a call center with centralized scheduling. It's been in development for 3 long years, as you just cannot implement this without first moving through the alignment continuum and building the required infrastructure. With over 80 different office locations, convenient care coordination has been a challenge. A call center allows that centralized capability to get the patient where he/she needs to be within the system at a glance and real-time. Coupled with a user-friendly EMR, there is no greater facilitator of a patient's ability to access care.

This stage is also indicative of mostly centralized functions in the group practices much like at the hospital. Human Resources, Marketing, Finance, and Information Technology all take place centrally with specialization in support of the physician group. Hopefully, the group has achieved the support of its own dedicated resources, not those provided sparingly by the hospital. Revenue cycle, posting, billing, and collecting all occur in a centralized environment aided by electronic practice management systems.

Physicians in this phase are largely employed under similar quality incentive metrics that can change from year-to-year based on committee or board-level support. Physician compensation will vary depending on specialty, but variation amongst like-specialists has been eliminated with differences occurring only due to productivity and quality-based metrics. Base contracts are the same, renewal periods are the same, non-compete clauses are the same. In short, contracting in this phase doesn't consume your life, nor do repeated returns to the negotiation table continue to shave away at your relationship with physicians. Not only does your relationship with physicians improve, your relationship with legal improves as each contract becomes more standard, reasonable, and customary, three words acting as "chicken soup" for the lawyer's soul.

Of course, this phase isn't a complete Utopia. Loss of autonomy and enhanced group dynamics certainly reduce individuality. If some modem of autonomy isn't preserved true entrepreneurs within the group won't flourish or prosper. Those rock stars in Phase One will feel constrained, stifled, and choked out from all the sameness around them. ***It's important in this phase to insist on standardization where it really matters and grant autonomy everywhere else.*** We perhaps heard it said best recently when discussing the virtues of fast food franchises with Akron celebrity and dignitary, Dr. Erwin Maseelall: Each locale may have its unique characteristics, but the fries all taste the same...

A standardized contract doesn't mean everyone should be paid the same. *Ensure capitalism rules and rewards go to the deserving.* Those with high volume *and* high quality should get paid more than those just punching the clock. Standardized processes around care transitions doesn't mean autonomy isn't preserved around medical decision-making. Integrated care delivery isn't the death of physician individualism when done correctly. It's harnessing the work of many individuals based upon best practices into a coordinated effort for the patient; and minimizing variation enough to enable the organization to professionally manage the size and scope created in Phase One.

Chapter 9. Maladies and Treatments

Physicians are a fascinating group to lead, and the alignment continuum is much easier to write about than to actualize. A basic dictum in medicine is that you need the right diagnosis to treat an illness, which in business correlates with identifying an issue's root cause. Next, we'll describe the three big "infirmities" we encountered in our multi-specialty physician group, shades of which probably exist in any organization, healthcare-related or not.

- United Nations Syndrome
- Paprikash Disorder
- Rapa Nui Phenomenon

These might sound unusual, but are all very real and can lead to pain, suffering, and an overall sickly system. They are usually indicative of larger organizational problems. Socrates said it best: "...the part can never be well unless the whole is well", and, as major transformative changes do not occur in a vacuum, systemic change should hopefully follow. In our case, the Tomahawk Leadership style began to infiltrate into other areas as its effectiveness became evident. It became a good example to emulate because it made sense. What follows are some ideas to address each malady.

United Nations Syndrome

United Nation's Syndrome indicates a lack of cultural identity. If a group resembles a myriad of independent states all competing for their own centric view of the world (the big WIIFM, or What's In It for Me), it's got United Nations Syndrome. The salient symptom is complete or partial failed implementation of centralized practices and policies aimed at improving the system as a whole. Typically, this is acted out passively. For example, you create a clear message, communicate it every way possible, and find three months later no one was listening. The immediate solution comes down to directed integration (revolutionary)---taking individuals and making them interact. The higher purpose of working together for the greater good of patient care comes later (evolutionary). The following are examples of what we did to create group identity, social investment, and common purpose in our multi-specialty physician group.

Abstract #17. Know thy neighbor. You can't refer to someone if you don't know they exist. We hosted a series of events and required attendance at meetings. It's the "mingle thing". Food and drink were provided to liven the social gathering. As doctors hate anyone telling them what to do, we didn't expect all to come, but most did. Also, we didn't prosecute those who failed to show. We just asked them why they didn't partake in the fellowship opportunity. We communicated the reasoning behind the expectation, and explicitly encouraged them to be there. The soft approach goes a long way.

Abstract #18. Advisory Committees. We developed small teams of physicians who met regularly to discuss group issues. Team composition was deliberate. Included were key physician leaders, both allies and, especially, the contrarians. We wanted to hear what they had to say, because that's what others were probably thinking--- valuable insight, indeed. We let them find solutions to their problems, and watched them gel in the process. We were there to listen, guide and learn.

Abstract #19. Internal Marketing. We took group pictures at the social events/meetings and standardized lab coats, business cards, and web pages with group identifiers and logos. Bikers, sports teams, and the military do it because it sends the same message: We are One. People enjoy being part of a club. We got marketing involved to internally advertise the group's doctors to each other as that was the initial target audience.

Abstract #20. Referral Pads. We deployed to all our provider offices "PPG Referral Pads" with all our physicians' contact info and all system testing sites. This was the preferred provider list from which referrals were suggested, always if ok with the patients and if clinically appropriate. We engineered it into our EMR, too. Here's how it works: If a patient needs a referral, the provider grabs the pad, circles a name, and hands it to the patient or front-desk. We emphasize to our doctors, "Keep patients in the system if it makes sense, and if it's

77

appropriate." *This is mostly for patients who need a new referral or want to switch providers. When we initially got resistance, we inquired why--- and here's where we discovered what docs thought about some of their colleagues, allowing us to address issues like: "Patient's hate him/her; never calls back; never sends a consult letter; nasty to me and my staff." It was our job as leaders to take that feedback back to the doctors, investigate, and act.*

Abstract #21. Out-of-System Referral Forms. We provided forms for written explanations and expected a call to the group's President for referrals out-of-system. Most doctors ignored this one, but it served to keep the concept top-of-mind. Again, we didn't harass those who didn't comply. We worked in the friction zone and tried to find the right balance between pushing and pushback. More importantly, we started developing the mindset of a contained-system. By keeping as much as possible in-house, the foundation was being set for following the patient throughout the continuum of care in value-based medicine.

Abstract #22. Mobile phones and Apps. We asked providers to directly communicate with each other regarding patient care if they weren't getting what they needed (something interns learn day One of residency). All provider mobile numbers were distributed amongst the group, and a HIPAA-compliant texting app was provided. We took every opportunity to drive the message home: "It's your responsibility to make things happen for your patient. You are all accountable to the patients and to each other". We constantly emphasized the "one group thing", and that, sometimes, personal intervention was necessary.

Paprikash Disorder

Paprikash Disorder is reflective of disparate contractual structures and misaligned compensation incentives. Be wary if you can't tell what's in your meal---good rule of thumb, right? Same goes for physician groups where everybody's contract may be different. Highly competitive environments result, out of necessity, in a multitude of physician alignment strategies:

Professional service agreements (leases), guaranteed models, wRVU models, and revenue-minus-expense models just to name a few, which we'll review in Chapter 11.

Even while rigidly staying within legal boundaries, aligning with physicians can still result in confusing financial engagements. The one economic principle that rings true beyond any other is that **Form Follows Financing**. If everyone in your group is behaving differently, you can't identify any true common motivation beyond delivering patient care, and you're having trouble moving toward your group objectives, you probably have Paprikash Disorder.

The solution is to strategically link compensation in a meaningful way. We provided structural encouragement for individuals to perform in a way that enhanced value in a group setting. In addition to the contract, we standardized, identified, and communicated minimum thresholds and expectations and backed those expectations with group transparency. Here are some ideas we employed.

Abstract #23. Move from guaranteed salary compensation models to ones that more closely align physicians with quality, efficiency, safety, patient satisfaction <u>and</u> productivity. Many of our contracts already had these elements, but if they didn't, we incorporated them as they came up for renewal. This is a transition which must happen. Some doctors don't like it because guarantees are great--- see one patient, see fifty, you get paid the same. Others, though, love the balanced approach to looking at them as a "complete doctor", where productivity alone often does not represent their whole story.

Abstract #24. Define what working "full-time" means. You'd be surprised at all the opinions you get on this once you start asking. We made it clear that if a provider's contract said "1.0 FTE", then he/she should be working every day. This is about patient access and living up to what they agreed when joining. Also, beware of the mysterious "administrative day". Our view on that was simple: If a doctor didn't have an administrative position, there was no administrative day. On this, be trusting but confirm. Don't prosecute but inquire. Physicians

81

are people with lives and families just like everybody else. We all have to leave work occasionally to take care of personal issues.

Abstract #25. Publish "leakage" information. By leakage we mean patients who get sent out of our health system. We provided un-blinded "out-of-system reports" for our PPG primary care doctors (physician names alongside the percentages). We got the usual, "The data is wrong" claim, but, ultimately, it proved directionally correct. The excitement died down after a few publications, as did the leakage out-of-system. Transparency works. Population health and care efficiency will be very difficult if patients and their information are disjointed.

Abstract #26. Release productivity information. We released monthly un-blinded wRVU (work relative value units) data to the group, just the raw numbers and variance from benchmark median. This initially provoked cries of indignation, especially from those with low numbers. Our response: "You're all part of one interdependent inter-related group. You are accountable to each other." Plus, we were just telling the truth, and the report was factual. Whenever challenged on the accuracy of the data, we were maniacal about investigating it. When we found errors, we corrected them. Our idea was to get in line with where the industry's going: Complete transparency.

Abstract #27. Publish quality information. We put that out there, too. Again, un-blinded, without editorial comments.

Abstract #28. Release office cancellation rates: We reported them out per physician, un-blinded. Upon first review, we were alarmed at the results. Quite frankly, we ourselves didn't believe the report, but it turned out to be true. Where we noticed unusual patterns, we spoke with the providers and office staff to understand what was happening on the ground. We heard stories that made perfect sense. Those that did not were immediately addressed. Unnecessarily canceling patients can be an access and patient satisfaction killer.

Abstract #29. Publish patient satisfaction data. We thought it important to let providers see what patients think about them. We did not release the verbatims, i.e., actual patient statements, because sometimes people can be just plain mean. Instead, we sent these sensitive remarks to the physicians individually. Where significant issues were identified, we spoke to the doctor in-person.

Abstract #30. Transition toxic, incorrigible, poorly performing providers out of the organization. We fired those who were incapable of change and suggested they work for the competition. It didn't matter if the doctor was a high-producer or in a tough-to-recruit specialty---we immediately started recruiting their replacement once these bad actors were identified. Permitting poor behavior or performance sends a very negative message to the rest of the physician group, as does not tolerating it.

The Rapa Nui Phenomenon

The Rapa Nui Phenomenon (RNP) alludes to an ancient people on Easter Island in the South Pacific who, according to legend, in fairly rapid fashion depleted the entire island of all natural resources in order to place very large stone heads in visible places. Why, nobody knows. In business, it manifests itself when someone or something has gained higher priority than solid business metrics can justify. If you find your organization's resources or strategies are overly devoted to any single person or entity at the expense of the rest, you may very well be experiencing RNP.

RNP often occurs when leverage is misaligned due to relationships or as a result of a highly competitive market. The problem may be complex but the solution is a combination of respect for human nature; trust in numbers; attention to logic; transparent decision-making; and communication. We constantly challenged ourselves to remain reality-based when approaching deals with physicians. Here's some "abstract business advice" we employed.

Abstract #31. Logically evaluate your investment in the physician or entity of concern and transparently communicate the findings to the rest of the executive team. Just take a deep

breath and start talking. You've got personal strength and data. Use them and give due respect to your proformas. Don't rationalize why they don't really capture the essence of a really special deal, and don't let others dismiss them.

Abstract #32. Avoid utopic portrayals of future state outcomes. We've all witnessed unreasonable arguments for a given project predicated on mostly desire, not facts. Within hospital systems you've got well-intentioned people helping people, which is a most noble endeavor. However, it's still a business. Make sure it's grounded in reality.

Abstract #33. Clearly identify objective criteria for success with each investment. This means keeping a close eye on the deal once inked. If it's working, great. If not, course correct rapidly. Multiple retro-fits will only add to your losses.

Abstract #34. Develop an exit strategy. Never enter a relationship you can't get out of. Build an exit strategy around objective criteria defined in your agreements (insist they are included) and hold fast during the negotiation phase. Here's where the go-arounds, emotions and drama surface. Be clear when negotiating that the deal has to work for both sides. If it doesn't, each should have the option to walk away from it. Too often physicians don't see that contractual out-clauses protect them, too. We tell them, "Do you really want to be stuck in a miserable deal for X number of years? I don't". If they still resist, walk away. Anyone who demonstrates undue unreasonable behavior during the negotiation phase of a contract signals trouble for the relationship ahead. They're either operating from ignorance or bad faith.

Chapter 10. The Ripley Effect

In 1861, Abraham Lincoln personally tested near the Whitehouse two guns that would revolutionize battlefield strategy and create a decided advantage for Union troops. They were breech-loading repeating rifles capable of shooting multiple times in rapid succession vs. the existing single-shot. Lincoln immediately recognized the value. Although revered as a visionary now, at the time his executive power was challenged via bureaucratic procedure and power politics.

General James Ripley, a 78 year-old bureaucrat, became concerned about the use of the new-fangled weaponry and the cost of using so many bullets. He was certain the troops on the ground would waste ammo if given the opportunity ("poor firing discipline"). This powerful administrator conducted a passive campaign of interruption and red tape. After 2 years of political grand- standing and delay tactics, the guns would reach the Union troops. Many historians credit General Ripley with causing thousands of unnecessary deaths and prolonging the Civil War. At this point you must be

thinking about your own General Ripley
experience.

In any company that has been around for longer
than three generations you will commonly find a
pervasive lack of creativity and entrepreneurism,
and a rigid reliance on structured bureaucracy.
The reason for that is simple: The company now
has more to lose than it has to gain and has shifted
from offense to defense. It's the organization's
version of basketball's illustrious four corners play
and is as true for healthcare systems as it is for
Blue Chips. The eventual outcome of this strategy
is the same for both. Your competitive lead
dwindles away to nothing, eventually placing you
in a self-created crisis that causes the team to
scramble in order to survive.

For young executives it can take several years to
realize what is happening. You propose a new idea
or even worse, an idea with a small element of risk
and then watch the ball be sent from one end of
the court to the other, never nearing the ultimate
objective. You'll watch as good ideas flounder
through Risk, Legal, Marketing, HR, then stall in
established committee structures only to emerge

late-to-market barely resembling the original idea. As such, when the unfortunate tendency for establishment-style behavior has taken root, dealing with it effectively will require that as a leader "You hold the Tomahawk".

Abstract #35. The Killer Asterisk. We've seen six months waste away while the inclusion of an asterisk was internally debated on an extremely important communication document.   An investment of millions within a system remained essentially a secret until the issue of the "damned asterisk" could be resolved. How did this happen? How could we let something so small have such a large impact? How did Lincoln allow his executive order to get thwarted in committee? It's simple. We gave the Tomahawk to someone else. What did we do? We called a meeting with those who needed to be there and in 15 mins solved the problem.

For many, this became a hard first lesson, but not the last, in the need for Tomahawk Leadership. Hospitals by nature are conservative, long-standing institutions with innate layers of risk avoidance and bureaucracy. The only way to successfully navigate the matrix is to realize that you own the problem. Put simply, other services and departments work for the organization to help push it forward. If you're the one accountable for outcomes, then they are accountable to you for their service and support---bring them to the table. And as leader, you can't wield the tomahawk if someone else is holding it.

This doesn't mean ignoring the perspective of your support peers. It means that you, the leader, control the throw and drive the decision. Other departments of course have great insight and disavowing them can be disastrous. Instead, it's your role to seek input, set timelines, and slice procedural apathy from pertinent subject matter. We are not recommending cavalier or reactionary decision-making. Your colleagues, subject matter experts, and reports should be used to help steady your aim, strengthen your hand, and see the target more clearly. Given the right circumstances, they may even convince you occasionally to *not* throw it.

The main point of this segment is that **you never hand over control of a decision for which you are accountable**.

Chapter 11. Alignment Models

Base Motivators

As mentioned in Chapter 6, "Flexibility, Adaptability, and Speed", correctly identifying the motivation behind a physician wanting to align with your organization and having models that provide the flexibility to adapt to their needs are key to successfully attracting physicians within your community. In our case, we didn't have much money to woo potential suitors, and, in a way, we're glad we didn't. It made us focus on what was really driving physicians rather than reverting to a more temporary gratifier--- Money. Having various models enables you to set up successful long-term relationships that meet both the needs of the organization and those of the physician.

Over the years we have successfully aligned with hundreds of physicians and physician groups in our community. This in turn has contributed in great part to the increase in accessibility of our service offerings to the community and in contribution margin to the system as a whole. Many may think that this can only be done by paying more for physicians than our competitors. As we've said previously, the truth is that while finances are important in any deal, it's rarely the main driver of a successful negotiation. Our path has been to create flexible employment and alignment alternatives that enable us to tailor each deal to the unique attributes and needs of the physician.

The key to this approach is correctly identifying the base motivation behind a physician seeking a closer relationship with the health system. Base motivations are important because they don't simply determine the success of the negotiation, they also determine the success of long-term alignment with the organization. Improperly identify a physician's base motivator, and you may soon find a misaligned physician practice and an unhealthy relationship.

Prior to identifying the main alignment models lets first look at 5 key physician base motivators we commonly see in the industry.

Security

Most physicians are driven by a need to practice medicine in a secure environment and, hence, are seeking you out to primarily gain a stable platform from which to accomplish that. The possible reasons they may be contemplating a change are numerous. Many buckle under the increasing burden of governmental regulations and/or don't have the resources to implement ICD-10, let alone purchase a meaningful use compliant EMR. Other physicians may be experiencing dropping volumes and finding themselves squeezed out due to changing referral patterns. Determining why they feel threatened is important to structure the right deal.

When security is the primary motivator, one option might be a median level guarantee model with proper safe guards around maintaining a reasonable level of productivity in the future.

Lifestyle

The motivation for physicians to attain work/life balance is a much more visible phenomenon today than in the good old days of medicine. We see it primarily in younger doctors or those with changing home dynamics. New rules governing residency work hours have provided some improvements to the learning environment, but they've also contributed to the re-setting of work-level expectations. More and more we're seeing CV's that state work/life balance as the #1 goal.

Perhaps the better compensation model here is a variable one which rewards them for the work they do, but protects the organization from over-compensation. Such is the case with a wRVU model (discussed later in this chapter). We are also very careful about what practice setting we recommend for them. As sometimes building and growing a practice is secondary, these doctors may actually flourish in an environment where patients come to them (urgent care clinics).

Academic/Leadership

The academician will come to the organization with a kilometric CV listing every personal accomplishment, sometimes going back to high school. They are motivated by engagement with residents, education, research, publications, altruism and prestige. It's important to recognize that they are indeed needed in any organization with teaching programs, and that's their preeminent mission: To teach. Said differently, you shouldn't overly push them into building market share or seeing large patient populations (although examples certainly abound of highly productive academic docs, financially-speaking)--- they would end up frustrated, and so will you, if you're measuring their success in terms of wRVU's.

The model and environment that might work best for them is one that rewards the achievements of research, certifications, and teaching duties. Hire right and hire for fit--- and the deal will work.

Entrepreneur

You'll know when you are engaging with an entrepreneur when they present you with a profit-and-loss statement rather than a CV.   They are motivated to align because they see the possibility for financial gain by joining an establishment. While these physicians seem on the surface to be primarily motivated by money, they are also driven by the need to create, build, and establish new programs. Appropriately align with these physicians or physician groups and they will become the rain makers of the organization. The key is to focus their motivation on something productive besides purely the financials. It's also important to employ them under a contract that keeps their base instincts intact.

Strangely enough, like their complete opposite lifestyle-motivated physician, a variable productivity model works best as it directly correlates with their effort. A Revenue Minus Expense model enables them to achieve financial success of their own making while keeping them aligned with the organization and unleashing them to build something better than they could have built on their own.

Autonomy

You will see various levels of need for autonomy amongst all physician types. However, if identified as *the* base need, you will need to be very careful in how you craft your employment agreement. Given the right model you can successfully align with physicians who require it. Done incorrectly, however, you will face constant challenges and conflict that threatens the core of the relationship. Truly autonomous physicians or physician groups usually need to be in control of more than just medical decision-making. These physicians desire involvement in staff hiring, regulatory compliance, billing, and IT selection. Whether they are good at these traditionally management-oriented roles isn't really the point, and we've seen both ends of the spectrum. In fact, most invariably think they are good at running a practice---- or at least better than you will ever be if you try to employ them. It's this very need to control the process that makes them poor choices for employment.

In these cases the best model may well be either a leased services arrangement or a clinically integrated one.

Taking into consideration the base motivators, our job is a practical one: To listen. When an unencumbered physician or physician group approaches us, the first question we ask is, "Tell us what you are looking for." We need to understand their needs, as that will inform what deal they'll be helping us to develop. Compensation will always be important, but, again, may not necessarily be the preeminent motivator. Recently we've seen many physicians from other systems abandon their employers due to feeling disrespected. Having a conversation about past experiences helps us comprehend their unique perspectives and avoid repeated disillusionment.

We've already said that physicians want to be left in peace to care for patients and get paid fairly. Here are the most common compensation models available. Some large multispecialty groups have a predilection for one; others have all types and combinations.

- **Guaranteed Model:** The physician is paid a set salary, which may or may not have certain productivity thresholds, which, if not met, may trigger adjustments. Usually seen in hospital-based positions where a certain number of physicians are needed for call coverage; also used when a new physician is brought to market to enable time to establish a practice, after which there should be a switch to a productivity model.

- **wRVU Model**: A variable productivity model where the physician gets paid a specific dollar amount per wRVU. As expenses fall to the organization, you've got to keep them tight.

- **Revenue Minus Expense Model**: This is the variable productivity "eat-what-you-kill" model. Here, the physician or group takes home whatever is left over after expenses have been deducted from earnings. As expenses fall to the doctor, it's in his best interest to keep overhead low.

- **Leased Model**: A physician group's services can be leased. The group's identity is intact, yet alignment exists along a Professional Services Agreement (PSA). Assets may be purchased. Staff may be leased or employed. Ancillary services and future cash flows may be purchased. There may even be the need for a co-management agreement if the group's operations are complex in size and scope. Expense allocation is contractually defined.

- **Clinical Integration:** Clinically integration can be very rewarding for physicians, health systems, and most importantly patients. It can apply to both employed and independent physicians. As an alignment model however, it is a great way to align independent physicians.

  The only thing better than an employed physician is one that isn't. If not forced by governmental payment modeling and a highly competitive landscape, the nirvana for hospitals and health systems would be to compete on quality service to both patients and physicians. All things being equal, independent docs participating within the framework of coordinated care provide the best care for patients. This can be a tremendous opportunity when you've got independent providers or groups that simply do not want to be employed. Hopefully, despite their need for autonomy, they'll see the opportunity and find value in participating within a larger framework. We've achieved clinical integration with independents using everything from programmatic leadership roles to true clinically integrated networks (CIN's) and Physician Hospital Organizations (PHO's). So, don't forget the importance of clinical integration as an alignment vehicle to engage independent physicians in your community. Don't let your own control issues get in the way. You'll still have to work diligently at building relationships and improving services for them and their patients, but the results can be very rewarding, and may even lead to other tighter alignment models in the future.

Of course, **all compensation arrangements have to be within fair market value (FMV) and memorialized legally in contracts.** You cannot just give a physician money--- there must be a contract. To determine FMV, use blended benchmarking data from commercial sources like Sullivan-Cotter or MGMA. Always have your legal and finance colleagues at your side and listen to them. If it's a large complex group acquisition, you should have a valuation company opine upon its worth, especially if an ancillary service purchase is part of the deal. Try to include in all contracts elements of productivity, quality and patient safety, and value realization.

As already alluded to, other important contractual considerations include time off; bonuses; leadership roles; academic needs; benefits; non-compete clauses. Again, make sure whatever you both agree upon fulfills the needs and expectations of both explicitly.

Lastly, perhaps one of the most overlooked alignment strategies is the one that is not contractual. Alignment begins with a good reputation and good relationship. Every doctor in the community is a potential alignment partner---keep that in mind as you go along your business and negotiate deals. It's worth repeating what we said earlier: *You are always being interviewed*.

Chapter 12. Results

- **25% decrease in out-of-system leakage**
- **41% increase in providers**
- **47% increase in our group's contribution to the health system's operating margin**
- **Top decile in physician engagement compared to both National Healthcare (91st %tile) and National Physician (90th %tile) Average (Press Ganey)**

These results are real and represent our present state as of this manual's publication, about 3 years into our administration. Positive changes in the first two led to an extraordinary increase in PPG's contribution to Akron General Health System's operating margin. **High physician engagement was the key.** That's the power of physician alignment done right. The impact was dramatically palpable after year 1 of our assuming leadership and applying the Tomahawk Leadership methods. As already mentioned, your organization will need to have a little faith and patience, both of which may at times be lacking as your team may be expected to work miracles. Here's where *you* need to have faith and stay the course. Just as you don't back down when you know you're right, you don't back down to the organizational naysayers. When the financials start looking good, they'll quiet down quickly. Of course, growth is expensive. Even after backing out the group's losses, the net contribution margin was still up by 41%.

PPG will soon reach over to 230 providers at over 80 locations. 28% are primary care, 72% are specialists. About 15% of the providers are advanced practice professionals. We employ 365 support staff, and the admin team consists of 30 people. The hospital system continues to enjoy positive margins after experiencing a multi-million dollar turn around attributable in large part to the group's help. PPG itself has set new financial records, the best in its history.

Competition from other systems is still fierce in our community, along with narrowing payer networks and statewide strategies that include never-before-seen levels of both vertical and horizontal integration. However, our clinical quality and financial performance have gained us a valuable world-class care partner, the Cleveland Clinic, in these regional and state efforts. Our future, once dim, is now very bright.

Outside of sheer growth and dollars, we have also made significant progress in behaving and operating like a team. We have successfully developed brand identity and internal group recognition. Leakage has been greatly reduced via operational standardization and the creation of group synergy and acknowledgement. We are now in the midst of implementing an EMR and will be transitioning to a single practice management system soon after. Efforts are on-going around revenue cycle standardization and access transformation as we continue to find ways to work in a more coordinated fashion for the good of the patient. We now have multiple recognized Patient Centered Medical Home practices and have joined the Cleveland Clinic's Quality Alliance, one of the country's largest CINs, capable of tracking and improving multiple quality metrics across populations.

Operational, quality, financial, and engagement scores are all moving with a purpose in a positive direction. PPG administration is now considered a good partner rather than a disinterested overlord, and our physicians and providers have the inter-active and attentive leadership they deserve. A recent Press Ganey study reflected this quite well. The group scored in the top decile for physician engagement when compared to national averages. Strong perceptions were found regarding respect, ethics, communication, teamwork, and relationships with administration. Verbatims (actual comments) relating to **"Quality of Leadership"** were telling:

- "Administration actually tries to make the lives of clinical staff members easier, not harder."
- "I have seen Akron General weather some difficult situations with integrity and honesty. The administration has my respect."
- "I like senior leadership in PPG."
- "I appreciate the open, honest, respectful communication between caregivers and administration."

The journey, however, is far from over. We are still in the middle of a healthcare revolution. By aggressively and nimbly running with tomahawk in hand, we at least now have steady footing over the moving ground beneath us. There's been no signal to refreeze our group just yet, and we are much healthier than we have been in a very long time.

We'd like to close this section with a few cautionary words. When employing the Tomahawk Leadership style, adjust its intensity to your own reality. Full-throttle Tomahawk Leadership is employed best when the situation is dire, organizational life or death---like what we had. It means pushing *everyone* around you really hard, really fast. You *will* develop some opposition. Hopefully, your results will garner support for continued action, but don't be surprised should pockets of organizational jealousy arise here and there, manifested usually in the form of passive-aggressive foot-dragging. "Nothing is more annoying than a good example", said Mark Twain. It's true. You're probably going to experience it, especially as your successes are celebrated.

Remember, too, early on you'll be criticized for not working miracles quickly enough. The praise-and-adulation phase comes later. Then, as conditions improve, people may forget the dark days past. Try not to let organizational amnesia get to you.

Beware of personal burn-out. The pace of this leadership style is not for the faint-hearted. It takes a lot of energy, drive and time to constantly be at it. Your life-work balance can very easily take a hit, so you've got to be maniacal about time management. Once you've gotten your group into a good groove, back off a little. If your team starts showing signs of fatigue, it's time to step back and re-evaluate where you are now vs. where you came from. Maybe it's time to lower the tomahawk. Don't put it away, but relax a little. Make sure to thank and reward those who followed you through this prolonged arduous campaign. A sure way to spawn apathy and lose good people is to drive them to exhaustion. When this happens, casualties follow. Appreciation, moderation and perspective keep a team together.

Lastly, what about the doctors and allied health professionals in our multi-specialty group? We really didn't talk much about them per se, except for the chapters on quality, alignment, group maladies and treatments. If you noticed, all we really did was bring them together. **We succeeded because of them, and we work for them.** We provided honest feedback and guidance. They did and continue to do the actual work of taking care of patients and have our deepest respect and admiration for their noble endeavors.

CONCLUSION

Tomahawk Leadership: A term which means comporting yourself with courage, a constant sense of urgency, truth and servant attitude. It's about dealing with problems head-on, not around them. It's about finding the shortest distance to an issue, and getting to the target quickly. It's about achieving results rapidly when the situation demands it. It's about personal involvement.

To attain extraordinary results in a short amount of time takes the extraordinary effort of many dedicated and gifted people, especially the doctors. Remember that you and your admin team will set the tone and example for how to prosecute the plan. Above all else, be honest and transparent with yourself, your team and caregivers.

It's been our observation that in most struggling companies, people are desperately looking for leaders who'll "tell it like it is" and take care of business. These are places in need of more tomahawk. It really comes down to this: Are you willing to do what it takes to get the job done? You have to start by deliberately disrupting the obvious obstacles and demonstrating resilience. This will create seismic ripples throughout the organization with some controversy and emotion, but consider it "controlled chaos" you'll have to manage. Fear not, good people will come to your side. In the end, every business endeavor has a responsibility to the people they serve, be they internal or external. You can't afford to fail them. Hopefully, turning around an organization or hospital system is more than just about your job or finances. Don't forget that it's really about the people and communities we serve.

About the Authors

Benito Alvarez MD, FACOG, MBA, CPE, JD, FACHE (pending) is an Ob/Gyn who throughout his career has held numerous leadership roles in major healthcare organizations, namely the Cleveland Clinic and Akron General Health System. He is presently Akron General's Senior Vice-President of Physician Alignment and President of Partners Physician Group. The son of Cuban refugees, he believed it his duty to join the US Air Force Reserves after the September 11th attacks, where he served as a flight surgeon and engaged in counter-intelligence activities.

In his spare time, he enjoys mountain climbing, weightlifting, shooting and riding his Harley-Davidson Softail. He is passionate about family, freedom, and, most importantly, helping people.

Jeffrey D. Pike, MHA, RN, NE-BC
graduated with a Bachelor's of Science in
Nursing at Kent State and with a Masters in
Health Care Administration from The Ohio
State University. Jeff has a long time career
in hospital administration, nursing
leadership, and service line development.
Jeff is currently Vice President of Akron
General's Partners Physician Group. He is a
passionate advocate of transformational
patient care, process efficiency, and
creating long term partnerships with
physicians.

In his spare time he teaches Masters level
courses at Akron University and Kent State.
He is also the recipient of Crain's Business
40 under 40 and Kent State's Barbara
Donaho Distinguished Leadership in
Learning Award.

Notes

Made in the USA
Lexington, KY
23 November 2017